The Army Library

MAIN
BATTLE TANKS

MAIN BATTLE TANKS

by John Nicholas

Rourke Enterprises, Inc.
Vero Beach, Florida 32964

Probably the most formidable and feared weapon in the modern army is the fast-moving battle tank, capable of inflicting terrible damage on enemy forces.

Library of Congress Cataloging-in-Publication Data

Nicholas, John, 1944-
    Main battle tanks/by John Nicholas.
    p. cm. — (The Army library)
    Includes index.
    Summary: Explores the different kinds of tanks and their military uses by various countries.
    ISBN 0-86592-420-1
    1. Tanks (Military science) — Juvenile literature. [1. Tanks (Military science)] I. Title. II. Series: Nicholas, John, 1944- Army library.
UG446.5.N47   1989   88-32727
358'.18 - dc19   CIP
                                                 AC

CONTENTS

NOV   1990

THE BIRTH OF THE TANK

The ancestor of the modern tank was probably a wooden chariot with four wheels used by the early Sumerians about 4,500 years ago. It was pulled by four horses and carried hide panels on the side as protection against spears. It was not until 1482, just ten years before Columbus sailed to America, that Leonardo da Vinci became the first man to devise an armored vehicle with slits for guns. Da Vinci was an Italian artist and scientist who designed many remarkable machines, including aircraft and helicopters.

The da Vinci "tank" did not get built. More than 400 years later, in 1855, James Cowan, an Englishman, designed a steam-driven vehicle with guns and a metal cover protecting the crew. It was condemned as "uncivilized." At that time machines for use in war were thought of as killing devices and not as a means of protection against enemy gunfire. By the start of World War One in 1914, however, people began to think differently.

One of the most famous tanks of all time, the M4 Sherman tank played a leading role in World War Two.

World War One quickly became a series of intense battles between armies of men stuck in long lines of trenches dug in the ground. Something was needed to protect men from heavy machine-gun fire and take guns close to the enemy trenches. The British were the first to build production-line tanks, and the first of these trundled into battle on September 15, 1916. The tank reached its target and took prisoner a number of terrified German soldiers.

The Sherman was well liked by its crew although its thin armor was vulnerable to the big German tanks and it had only a 75mm gun.

A Sherman tank dramatically shows its ability to throw flame across a large distance, igniting bushes and shrub or enemy vehicles. ▼

By the end of World War One in 1918, the tank had become an important fighting machine. Tank fought tank, and new designs increased performance. World War Two started with an attack by large numbers of German tanks and planes against Poland, in eastern Europe, on September 1, 1939. The tank played a major role in what the Germans called **blitzkrieg**, which means "lightning war."

When the war started, the most powerful German tank weighed 19 tons, was 18 feet long, and had armor up to 1 inch thick. By the end of the war in 1945, the Germans were operating 68-ton tanks, 24 feet long, with 6-inch armor. The size of a gun, given in millimeters, is measured in terms of the interior diameter of the barrel. This measurement is known as the **caliber**. Between 1940 and 1945 the caliber of the tank had gone from a standard 37mm to 88mm. World War Two saw many big tank battles, primarily between German and Russian forces in the Soviet Union and eastern Europe. The greatest battle of all involved 6,000 Russian and German machines in a gigantic clash near the Russian town of Kursk in July 1944.

A group of M60 battle tanks stops for orders on a military exercise.

During this period American tanks were generally much smaller and weighed less. They were built for speed and had light armor. The Russian tanks were heavily armed and armored. Over 9 inches of steel covered the JS-111, which had a 122mm gun. The most famous American tank during World War Two was the Sherman, produced in many different versions. A typical Sherman had 3-inch armor, a 75mm gun, a top speed of 25 MPH, and a weight of 30 tons.

The Sherman was well liked by its crew but it had thin armor that was vulnerable to the heavy guns of the giant German Tiger tanks. Britain produced a range of tanks during the war, from the small 7-ton Tetrarch to the 40-ton Churchill tank equipped with a 75mm gun. During World War Two, armies learned the importance of heavily armed tank units. They were the only fighting machines that could advance at high speed, protect gun crews, and penetrate enemy positions with a more than even chance of surviving. After the war, which ended in 1945, even more importance was placed on the tank in battle.

The tank's ability to move rapidly across ground and support infantry units taking enemy positions has been an important aspect of military power for more than fifty years.

THE MODERN BATTLE TANK

Although its weapons have become more powerful since World War Two and its firepower much greater, the job of the modern battle tank is not very different from what it was at the end of World War Two. That job is to knock out other tanks and to take rapid control of large areas of land that might otherwise be occupied by the enemy. Yet the technology has changed completely. In World War Two the tank was a fairly simple vehicle, while today the tank is a very complex and highly sophisticated machine. It has advanced electronics, powerful computers, and highly trained personnel.

The three main requirements of a tank are difficult to meet in one vehicle. First, it must carry a very powerful gun with as much ammunition as possible. Second, it must be highly mobile and quick over rough ground, with a good range on internal fuel tanks. Third, it must be able to survive in battle. This means it must not only resist attack by protecting its own vital parts with armor, but it must also protect its crew members, who are essential for its job.

The T48 series of main battle tanks was developed in the 1950s and over 11,700 were built before production ceased in 1959.

Improvements made to tank engines has increased their efficiency on the battlefield and allowed them to take advantage of new gun technology. ▲

Even armored personnel carriers and light tanks take their place on the battlefield, and must be able to cross rivers and shallow water.

A tank is driven ashore from a utility landing craft during a joint U.S./Spanish military exercise in October 1983.

Sometimes these design features are balanced against each other to produce a tank for a specific need at a particular time. For instance, during the 1950s western tanks needed powerful 120mm guns to knock out the heavily armored Soviet tanks if they ever fought against each other. These guns were very heavy, and armored protection had to be kept to a minimum. So the U.S. Army's M103 tank was designed with a powerful 120mm gun but lacked speed because the engines of the day were not powerful enough for the tank's weight.

When technology produced lighter guns and materials, armored protection was easier to achieve while still providing high firepower. Improvements in engine technology gave the tank more performance and range. In turn, this enhanced the ability of the tank to fight and survive. Today, with tanks like the M60 and the M1 Abrams, the army has advanced fighting machines with high performance.

Great advances have been made with tank engines. The British Chieftain appeared in the 1960s with an engine capable of running on several different types of fuel. This was useful, because in wartime supplies of a particular fuel might be scarce. Moreover, the engine could be quickly removed and replaced. This is also an important asset where time is of the essence. A disabled tank would not survive for long.

In the 1960s, a typical tank diesel engine produced 650 horsepower and gave a fuel consumption of 9 miles per gallon. Today, a modern tank diesel engine delivers 1,500 horsepower and gets 12 miles to the gallon. The performance of tank engines has increased greatly, while the weight of modern tanks has increased only slightly compared with those of the 1960s. This gives the engine even greater efficiency.

Tanks are designed with water-tight hulls and road and running wheels that allow the vehicles to cross rivers or streams.

Some tank designers are trying to get even more performance out of tank engines. They have fitted a gas-turbine device to a standard diesel engine. The diesel provides power for normal running and the turbine is switched on for higher performance in combat. Some modern tanks, such as the M1, have powerful gas-turbine engines. These use a lot of fuel and put so much heat through their exhaust pipes that it is dangerous for people or other vehicles to get too near the rear of the tank when the engine is running. The best design for the future seems to be a combination diesel and turbine engine.

Apart from its conspicuous gun, the most obvious features of a tank are its tracks. These are essential for

Because tanks are limited in range by the fuel they can carry, these battle vehicles are frequently moved around on trailers or rail cars.

running over rough ground, knocking down walls, or simply climbing over the back of other traffic that gets in the way. Tracks are one of the most important aspects of tank design. They must be reliable and efficient, giving the tank good handling. Tracks must be durable and not easily broken. They must, ideally, be as quiet as possible. The loudest sound a tank makes is sometimes the noise of its tracks across the ground.

Tank repair and maintenance is important both for combat readiness and for high levels of performance in battle.

Tanks' tracks are vital to their movement, and must be designed for maximum efficiency and reliability. ▼

Since World War Two, tanks have been used in all types of terrain and in many different climates, fighting battles in mud-soaked plains and hot, humid deserts.

Tanks move when power from the engine is connected to the drive wheels. The drive wheels have sprockets that connect to links in each track. If the wheels are not correctly designed, the power from the engine will not be transmitted with maximum efficiency. The tank moves across the ground on road wheels whose only purpose is to spread the load and keep the tracks positioned on either side of the tank body.

Tracks receive hard use and must often be replaced. The tracks on the M1 have a life of less than 1,400 miles. Track life varies widely and depends to a great extent on the overall design of the vehicle. The German Leopard 2 has a track life of more than 4,600 miles. Some tanks have rubber pads to cut road noise, and others have special shoes for snow and ice to help them grip better and prevent the tank from sliding.

A West German Leopard tank on the firing line in a competition in Canada during 1983.

Tanks sometimes have to cross rivers, and most tanks today are designed to be **amphibious.** They can move on dry land or underwater, crawling along from one side of a river to the other. Being amphibious permits the tanks to keep moving forward without waiting for army engineers to build bridges. When fording a river, the tank is sealed so that water will not leak into vital parts. The air sealed inside gives it buoyancy in the water. This tendency to float means the tank loses grip on the riverbed. The turning tracks propel the tank forward. A submerged tank could get bogged down in the mud unless the crew was sure the river bed could support its weight.

In addition to having high firepower, mobility, and good protection, a tank must not be too large. Tanks are moved frequently, often by train, ship, or another road vehicle. When they operate on exercise in peace time, they must use ordinary roads and railways. A tank's size must never exceed the maximum permitted dimensions set down for freight.

17

GUNS AND ARMOR

An M1 Abrams main battle tank of the 11th armored cavalry regiment reacts to an alert on the East/West German border.

Since World War Two, tank designers have been running an unending competition between firepower and armor. As guns have become bigger and more powerful, protective armor has had to improve to keep up with the added penetration of explosive shells. At the end of World War Two, the largest gun in production used for tanks was the 88mm of the German Tiger 2. Since the end of the war in 1945 the Soviets have led the way in bigger and more powerful guns.

First deployed in 1950, the Soviet T-54 became the first production tank to mount a 100mm gun. In 1963, the Soviet army received the first of its T-62 tanks, which had a 115mm gun. Then in 1974 came the T-74 with a 125mm gun. The standard United States Sherman tank of World War Two had a 75mm gun. In response to the increase in Soviet gun caliber, the M47 medium tank was introduced in 1952 with a 90mm gun. This was followed by the M60 with a 105mm gun in 1960. The M1 has a similar caliber.

Tanks are designed and specially built not only to fire shells and destroy enemy positions but to survive in the heat of battle.

Tanks "fight" in a mock battle during combined U.S./Japanese training exercises in Yokota, Japan. ▼

The tank gun can be mounted in either one of two ways. In the most commonly used design, the gun is fixed in a turret so that it can only move up and down. This is called **elevation**. The turret rotates on a mounting that is attached to the body of the tank. Fixed in the turret, the gun can pivot to the left or right. This pivoting movement is called **azimuth**. By controlling elevation and azimuth, the gun can point in any direction.

The alternative method of mounting the gun is to attach it rigidly to the main body of the tank and do away with the turret. This means the gun can move in elevation but not in azimuth, so the tank itself must point directly at the target. Moreover, the gun cannot be fired with the tank on the move. That is a big disadvantage, although the Swedish S tank was built like this. The only real advantages are that the gun can be loaded automatically and the tank is much lighter. Automatic loaders are faster than manual loaders, but the bulky equipment cannot be fitted inside a turret.

The arrangement and design of the body of a tank and its turret is a reflection of how the designer sees the tank being used. The Soviets see the tank as a weapon for quick strikes across large areas in mass attack at high speed. In the West, the tank is regarded as a weapon for stopping these massive assaults. Western tanks place more emphasis on being able to hide, lie in wait for an attacker, and fire from fixed positions.

Although tanks may appear cumbersome, achieving their objectives by brute force, precision design and engineering is ▶ *an important part of making them work effectively.*

The M551 Sheridan tank was designed to fire both conventional shells and missiles from its 152mm barrel.

Soviet tanks have well-rounded turrets that deflect shells. This shape, however, prevents the gun from making large up and down movements. This does not matter so much to the Soviets because their tanks would fire on the run across wide-open spaces. Western tanks have guns attached to squat turrets in such a manner that they can be pointed down as well as up. This allows tank drivers to place their vehicles in depressions or hollows in the ground with the front of the tank pointing slightly upward. To fire forward, the gun would have to be pointing down with respect to the body of the tank. In this way, western tanks can carry out the defensive role their commanders prefer.

Modern tanks carry three main types of ammunition for use with the main gun. This ammunition has the single objective of attacking other tanks and either destroying or disabling them. One type is called **armor-piercing-fin-stabilized-discarding-sabot (APFSDS) ammunition**. It was first developed in World War Two as an armor-piercing device. It consists of a steel shaft, sharpened to a point at the front end with fins attached at the other end. Because the device is so much smaller in diameter than the caliber of the gun, it is held in place by a protective case, called the **sabot**, which is jettisoned when the device is fired from the barrel.

The APFSDS is made from tungsten, one of the hardest metals known. Tungsten can survive temperatures up to 16,100°F. When the pointed armor-piercing shaft reaches the target, in this case a tank turret, it punches a hole through the steel casing and ricochets around inside, doing considerable damage to crew and equipment. The second type of ammunition is called **high-explosive-anti-tank (HEAT) ammunition**. It is a specially shaped explosive charge within a case that detonates just before it strikes the target. Inside the shell the charge is shaped like a cone, which focuses the explosion into a narrow jet that easily penetrates thick armor.

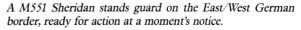

Camouflage is important for tanks that must sometimes lie hidden for hours or even days to ambush enemy forces.

A M551 Sheridan stands guard on the East/West German border, ready for action at a moment's notice.

An M1 Abrams main battle tank fires its gun under simulated battle conditions on a U.S. Army training ground.

The third type of tank ammunition is the **high-explosive-squash-head (HESH)** type. When the explosive hits the target it flattens out like a cake and then detonates. All this happens in a fraction of a second, but when the charge explodes it shatters scraps of metal from inside the turret and the energy sends them hurtling around at high speed. This would be fatal for the crew and lethal for the tank.

Other ammunition is carried by a tank to attack infantry and foot soldiers. It is used in machine guns attached to the tank at various locations, including the top of the turret and the driver's position. As tanks are becoming increasingly threatened by slow, low-flying aircraft and helicopters, tank designers are thinking about ways to arm them with light missiles for defense. The French in particular are working in this area.

Defensive armor has usually been made from steel plate with nickel-chrome for strength. In the 1970s, British researchers in Chobham, England, developed what most experts believe is the best tank armor ever devised. Called **Chobham armor,** it is highly secret but is believed to consist of several layers of different materials spaced at crucial distances in such a way that they defeat almost all forms of **anti-tank shell**.

A night shot of an M1 firing its main gun highlights the enormous fire power of the modern tank. ▲

The most recent development in tank protection is to arrange a series of explosive panels around the outside of the tank. These detonate outwards when hit by incoming shells. They do no damage to the tank but totally disrupt the explosive spread of the shell.

The M551 is considered a light tank, which operates on the edge of the battlefield and in areas where the enemy may be hiding.

TANKS IN SERVICE

The United States Army operates about 13,300 battle tanks, a force made up of three different types of tanks. These are the M48, the M60, and the M1 Abrams, the latest and the most powerful. By comparison, the Soviets have about 53,300 tanks. Until recently, Soviet tanks were generally considered to have greater firepower than their United States equivalents, but the introduction of the powerful Abrams has helped to restore the balance.

The M48 was first deployed with the army in 1953. Since that time, it has seen service with the armies of seventeen countries outside the United States. Chrysler was selected to build this tank in 1950, and about 1,450 are still in service with the U.S. Army. Many have been converted to other duties, including a bridge-laying version able to span gaps up to 60 feet in width.

Equipped with a 105mm gun, the M48 has had a long and distinguished career since its first appearance in the early 1950s.

◄ *Modern tanks must be moved by air to reach distant battlefields quickly and in good fighting condition*

This M48A3 carries an internal load of 62 rounds of ammunition for its 90mm gun. ▼

The M48 entered service with a 90mm gun, but has been fitted with a 105mm gun to update it. The hull is made up of cast armor, as is the turret. The driver is seated at the front of the hull with three other crew members in the turret. The commander and gunner are on the left, and the loader sits on the right. A special fireproof bulkhead separates the fighting section, composed of the driving position and turret, from the rear-mounted diesel engine. The engine delivers 750 horsepower and has a top speed of 30 MPH.

With a length, including the main gun, of 24 feet and a width of almost 12 feet, the M48 is 10 feet high and weighs 52 tons. It has a range of 288 miles and carries two machine guns. One is mounted on top of the turret. The M48 has done well in action, and it has seen combat in Korea, Pakistan, and the Middle East, where the Israeli army have used it in many operations.

During the late 1950s engineers gave an M48 a new engine and carried out tests on it. This work resulted in several modifications. The Soviets had introduced a new tank gun with a larger caliber and improved firepower; it was necessary for American tanks to match that. Military designers decided to base the new tank on the M48 but add a new 105mm British gun; it was called the M60. The M60 tank had a number of major improvements, and more than 10,600 were built between 1960 and 1985.

Beach landing exercises under conditions that may be found anywhere in the world are a vital part of battle readiness.

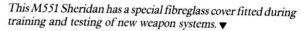

This M551 Sheridan has a special fibreglass cover fitted during training and testing of new weapon systems. ▼

▲
This picture shows gun trials of special tank weapons attached to a standard M60 chassis.

An M48 equipped with a 105mm gun, for which it carries an internal load of 54 rounds, stands ready for shipment with its gun traversed to the rear. ▼

The new engine fitted to the M60 was a 750-horsepower, 12-cylinder diesel, but although efficiency was improved the top performance remained about the same as the M48. The bigger gun, however, increased the gross weight to about 57 tons. Although the hull remained the same length, overall length including the gun was 31 feet. At one point a much bigger 152mm gun was fitted, giving the M60 the ability to fire shells or launch missiles through the barrel. The idea was good, but it failed to work out and many problems were encountered before that model was abandoned.

The original M60 was replaced in 1962 by the M60A1 model, which had a redesigned turret and a new hull. The M60A2 was the version with the 152mm barrel that was abandoned. The M60A3 that followed has many improvements. The gun is now stabilized by control systems that keep the barrel pointing at a specific target despite the attitude the main body of the tank might take as it rolls over rough ground. Special devices have been added for sighting the gun at night, as have smoke discharges that create an enveloping blanket of smoke within which to hide.

Special sighting devices and electronics inside the tank turret dramatically improve the accuracy and fire power of these fighting vehicles compared to their World War Two predecessors.

The M60 carries 63 rounds of 105 ammunition and a total 6,850 rounds for the two machine guns. This all-round tank is well recognized as a versatile fighting vehicle with good firepower and robust construction. These factors are important for the crew that have to spend their working lives living and riding mechanical battlewagons. Fourteen countries operate the M60, and the type was still in production for export orders at the end of 1988.

The M60A3 became the standard configuration for this tank, and the army now has about 7,500 in service. Of these, more than 5,600 are M60A1 versions modified to bring them up to the level of the production A3 model. Many different duties have been identified for versions of the M60, including bridge-laying, bulldozing, demolition, and crane work.

In searching for a major replacement for the M60 series, the U.S. Army turned to a cooperative project with West Germany on the MBT-70, which stood for Main Battle Tank 1970. The work came to nothing, though, and the U.S. eventually fell back upon a different plan for the M60. The M1 Abrams was built in the United States. Its first derivative was the M1A1.

Although parked here for public viewing, tanks frequently park on sharp inclines to raise their guns for firing on targets over ridges or other obstacles.

An M60 tank unit trains in forest areas for battles in wooded terrain.

The Abrams is a major step forward for American tank builders. It is a revolutionary design with special armor and a powerful, 1,500-horsepower gas-turbine engine. This gives the Abrams a top speed of 45 MPH and a range of about 320 miles. The tank is 32 feet in length, including the gun, with a hull length of 26 feet. It is 12 feet wide and has a height of 9 feet, 6 inches — 12 inches lower than the M60 series. This is an important feature, because reduced height means the frontal area of the tank is less exposed to enemy fire and possible damage. The M1 weighs more than 60 tons and is the heaviest U.S. tank ever.

The main armament for the Abrams is the 105mm M68 gun. Three machine guns are positioned at various locations. Six smoke dischargers are located on each side of the turret, which is very angular and not rounded like the turret of the M60. The hull and turret is protected with British Chobham armor, which its designers say will protect the vehicle against most anti-tank shells.

Many different types of support vehicles frequently gather for tests and simulated combat, rehearsing activities they would carry out during a war.

The M1 requires a crew of four to operate. The driver sits in front in the fixed portion of the hull. In the turret, the commander and the gunner sit on the right and the loader sits on the left. The M1 has special compartments around the inside walls of the turret for shells and ammunition. It carries about 55 rounds of 105mm ammunition and a total 12,400 rounds for the three machine guns.

Special blow-out panels forming the outer edge of the turret ensure that if a shell hits the turret, the explosion is channeled outward and not into the crew compartment. Blow-out panels are designed so that if they are hit by exploding shells the energy causes them to push out rather than fold in. This offers a degree of protection because it deflects the explosive energy of the shell away from the interior. Similar panels protect the fuel tanks.

For a massive steel fighting vehicle on tracks, the M1 has an impressive turn of speed. Accelerating from a standing start to 20 MPH in seven seconds, the tank can charge across country at 30 MPH or race along paved roads at 45 MPH. The controversial turbine engine can run on gas, diesel, or jet fuel, a handy flexibility where fuels can get scarce. The engine has been criticized, however, as being unnecessarily expensive to run because it uses extra fuel unless running at top speed.

▲
An M1 Abrams meets an M2 Bradley armored fighting vehicle during exercises in July 1985.

The M1 Abrams has had a mixed reception in the U.S. Army; some people feel that its engine is not reliable enough for the tough conditions of modern combat. ▼

The M1 has a combat weight of more than 27 tons and carries a crew of four; special compartments on the inside of the turret ▶ house shells and ammunition.

From a standing start the M1 can accelerate to 20 MPH in seven seconds and reach a speed of 45 MPH along ordinary roads. ▼

When the tank is charging across country, it can aim and fire its gun on the run. This is made possible by a fire control system that uses lasers to provide information for computers to work out instructions for the gun, which is then aligned and fired on command. The laser ranging system is in common use with many tanks has been developed over the years into a highly reliable and important piece of equipment.

The laser device sends a beam of invisible light from the tank to the target. The gunner can point the beam within a wide range of view and select the specific target from inside the turret as he looks through an eyepiece connected to a small telescope that presents a view of the scene outside. The gunner then uses the laser beam to provide instructions to the computer about the range to the target. This is achieved when the laser bounces off the target and is reflected back to a special sensor on the tank.

The computer is fed this information and calculates the precise angle at which the barrel of the gun must be positioned to get a direct hit on the target. The gunner then pushes the firing switch and the round is fired. Equipment like this is very expensive, but it is essential for accurate aim and fire. The M1 can carry out these functions at high speed across rough ground. This gives it an advantage because it is more difficult for the enemy to hit a fast-moving target.

When the M1 was designed in the early 1970s, the contract to build the tank was given to Chrysler Defense, Inc. This company was taken over by General Dynamics in 1982. The army wants approximately 7,500 Abrams battle tanks, and by 1988 about 4,500 were in use. Production began in 1979 at the Lima Army Tank Plant in Lima, Ohio, and it will be some time before all orders are filled. Although the M1 has had its fair share of criticism from people who believe it is too big and too expensive, the Abrams will be the main army battle tank for the next twenty years — and perhaps longer.

ON THE BATTLEFIELD

The United States Army has about 13,300 battle tanks, and the Soviet Union has approximately 53,300. The true balance between the two countries, however, is not as straightforward as a simple game of numbers. The United States is a strong partner in the **North Atlantic Treaty Organization (NATO)**. NATO was formed in 1949 as a defense alliance between the U.S., Canada, Iceland, Great Britain and eleven other European countries. Direct comparison between tank forces must also take account of the NATO partners and their tanks.

In the unhappy and tragic event of a major war with a country like the Soviet Union, it is unreasonable to imagine the U.S. having to face battle without her NATO partners. The tank forces of NATO countries are an important contribution to the balance of power. Together, these NATO countries field about 17,200 tanks. Added to the United States tank force this provides a total 30,500. This total is still less than the Soviet tank force, but it is not nearly so imbalanced as it seems at first. There is, however, another catch here.

▲

Tanks are designed to protect each other and only operate alone when absolutely necessary.

A World War Two Sherman tank is well hidden among the rust red leaves of these trees.

Although at first sight it may appear chaotic, a tank battle has a specific attack or defense plan and each tank is assigned a position on the battlefield. ▼

The Soviet Union is also part of a defense alliance, the **Warsaw Pact**. In addition to the Soviet Union, the Warsaw Pact consists of six countries in East Europe. The Soviet Union plays a major controlling influence in the defense forces of the Warsaw Pact. Together, they operate 14,600 tanks which, added to the Soviet tanks, provides a total of 69,900.

Most Warsaw Pact tanks are old and vulnerable to attack from modern weapons. Some date back to World War Two, while most are from the 1950s and 1960s. They would not survive long on the battlefield. Only 23,000 Soviet and Warsaw Pact tanks are less than twenty years old. This is only one-third of their total tank force. By comparison, 19,100 NATO tanks, two-thirds of the total force, are less than twenty years old. In addition, NATO has a large number of anti-tank weapons to destroy large numbers of armored vehicles quickly.

Most NATO countries are directly in the firing line, if any country in the alliance were to mount a surprise attack on the Soviet Union. Any major land battle in Europe would bring widespread devastation of people, property, and land. With this in mind, NATO forces are defensive forces, because nothing could be gained by starting aggressive military operations.

▲
Under active combat no tank would intentionally display the national flag in this bold fashion, but on exercises it is a useful way of distinguishing "friend" from "foe".

A complex and sophisticated system of signals and messages helps coordinate tank operations involving several hundred ▶ battle vehicles.

It is a basic rule of war that attacking forces need at least three times the firepower of defensive forces to push through an assault and win. Attacking armies on the move in open country, advancing against hidden guns and protected command centers, must expect to lose a lot of men and machines to enemy fire. The Soviet and Warsaw Pact forces could not mount a strike attack on the West with a sure guarantee of winning. So long as NATO keeps up a strong guard, the odds are too great for any military alliance to think it can win.

▲
Tank crews take a break during simulated combat exercises in Canada involving U.S. M60 battle vehicles.

Only the tank can move quickly across roads, fields, and rough trackways and remove most obstacles standing in its path. ▼

◄ Tank crews must always try to keep their vehicles together; lone tanks and small groups are vulnerable to enemy forces.

The main opposition to NATO tanks would be the Soviet T-64, T-72, and T-80 battle tanks. The T-64 appeared in the 1960s and about 8,000 are in service with the Soviet army. It has not been exported to Warsaw Pact countries. The tank has a total length of 30 feet, with a top speed of more than 40 MPH and a range of 280 miles. It carries a 125mm gun and a crew of three. the T-72 is slightly bigger, heavier, and slower than the T-64 but carries a similar gun. This tank has been exported to several pro-Soviet countries in the middle East.

A squadron of tanks moves up rapidly on orders from the front line.

The T-80 has been kept as disguised as possible by the Soviet Union, and very few have been seen close up by Westerners. Like the Abrams, it is powered by a gas-turbine engine and is thought to have a top speed of 47 MPH with a range of 230 miles. At 47 tons, the T-80 is the heaviest of all three types. The T-80 resembles the T-64 in some ways, although it has better armored protection and is likely to suffer less from NATO anti-tank weapons than the other Soviet tanks.

NATO countries primarily operate the American M48 and M60 tanks and the very effective Leopard and Chieftain tanks. The Leopard series is German, and that country currently operates about 2,400 Leopard 1 tanks and 1,500 Leopard 2 tanks. The Leopard 1 is about twenty years old and carries a 105mm gun. It has a length of 31 feet, weighs 44 tons, and has a top speed of 40 MPH.

The Leopard 2 is bigger. Including the gun, its total length is 32 feet, but the hull is 2 feet longer than Leopard 1's hull. The Leopard 2 joined the German army in 1980. It weighs 60 tons and carries a 120mm gun. Developed by the German firm of Rheinmetall, the gun is also being fitted to later versions of the M1A1 Abrams. Top speed for the Leopard 2 is 45MPH, and the tank has a range of 340

miles. It is better protected that the Leopard 1 and has improved handling over rough country.

The British Chieftain also uses a 120mm gun and is one of the biggest tanks of all. Length is more than 35 feet, and the tank weighs 60 tons. A derivative, called the Challenger, is 38 feet long and weighs more than 68 tons. A total of 64 shells and 4,000 rounds of ammunition for two machine guns are carried in the turret, and the tank has full fire control systems enabling it, like the Leopards, to fire on the run under any battlefield condition, day or night.

Short of nuclear war, the main battle tank is probably the most feared weapon of war on land. It alone can wreak havoc over several hundred square miles in a single day. As history has shown, massed tank divisions in full flight across open country can seize control of the battle, opening up enemy terrain for infantry and **armored personnel carriers** to pour through. Combined with air power, tank forces are a formidable threat. It is the fear of this *blitzkrieg* style of warfare that has led American and NATO forces to equip their ground forces with effective anti-tank weapons capable of blunting the edge of a massive surprise attack.

A UH-1 helicopter modified to look like a Soviet helicopter and an M551 Sheridan modified to resemble a Russian troop carrier are used in simulated exercises against Soviet forces.

GLOSSARY

Amphibious	A vehicle designed to float on water or drive across land.
Anti-tank shell	A shell designed to break open the protective armor of an enemy tank.
APFSDS ammunition	Armor-piercing-fin-stabilized-discarding-sabot, consisting of a steel shaft, sharpened to a point at the front end with fins attached to the other end.
Armored personnel carriers	Tracked or wheeled vehicles protected with armor plate and used to carry soldiers or infantry men.
Azimuth	Movement to left or right in a horizontal direction.
Blitzkrieg	The German word for lightning war, the name given to surprise attack involving ground attack planes and tanks.
Caliber	The diameter of the inside of the barrel of a gun indicating the power of the artillery piece.
Chobham armor	A special type of armor developed at a British research institute in Chobham, England. Chobham armor has proved resistant to all types of conventional anti-tank ammunition.
Elevation	Movement up or down in a vertical direction.
HEAT ammunition	High-Explosive-Anti-Tank ammunition. An explosive charge that detonates just before it strikes the target to provide maximum effect.
HESH ammunition	High-Explosive-Squash-Head ammunition. A type of ammunition designed to flatten like a cake as it hits the target and detonates to shatter scraps of metal inside the turret.
North Atlantic Treaty Organization (NATO)	An alliance of the U.S., Canada, and 11 West European countries operating under a military pact to support one another; an attack on one is considered an attack on all.
Sabot	A protective case, designed to fill out the space between a shell and the interior of the barrel.
Warsaw Pact	A mutual defense organization created in 1955 by the communist countries of Eastern Europe. It provides a unified military command among the member countries and allows Soviet units to be stationed inside the borders of the other member countries; the organization is an equivalent of NATO.

INDEX

Page references in *italics* indicate photographs or illustrations.